Coloring & Activity Book

SUPER JUMBO

COLORING

KAPPA Books
A Division of KAPPA Graphics, LP

THE COW JUMPED OVER THE MOON.

SLEEPY MOON

MAMA BEAR

FUNNY CLOWN

SILLY RIDE

A FEAST!

MY HOUSE IS MADE OF STRAW.

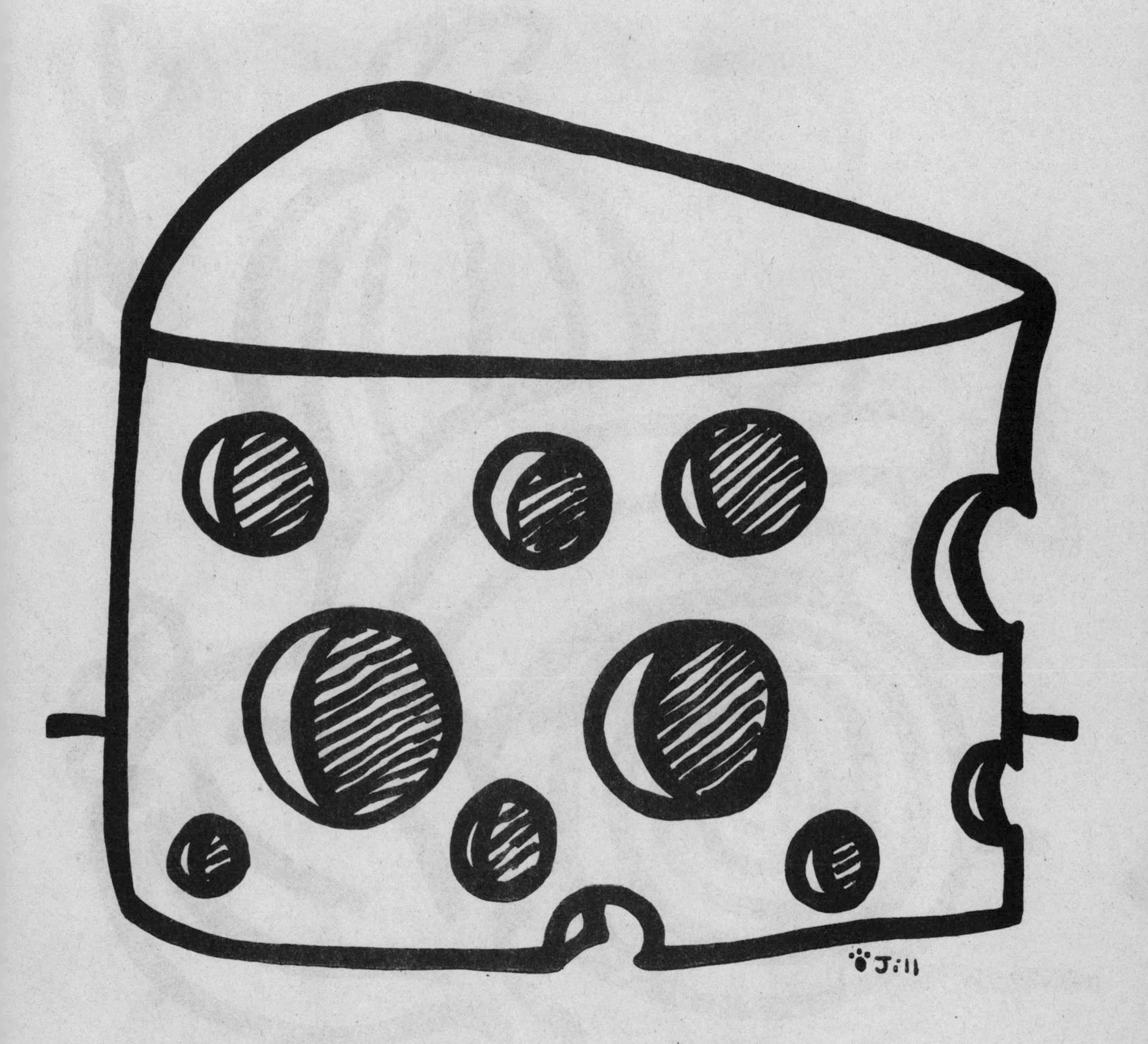

SWISS CHEESE

HOT ONIONS

SALTY PRETZELS

GOING SHOPPING!

THANKSGIVING DAY QUEST

NAME THE FRUITS

MY FAVORITE CEREAL

CONNECT THE DOTS!

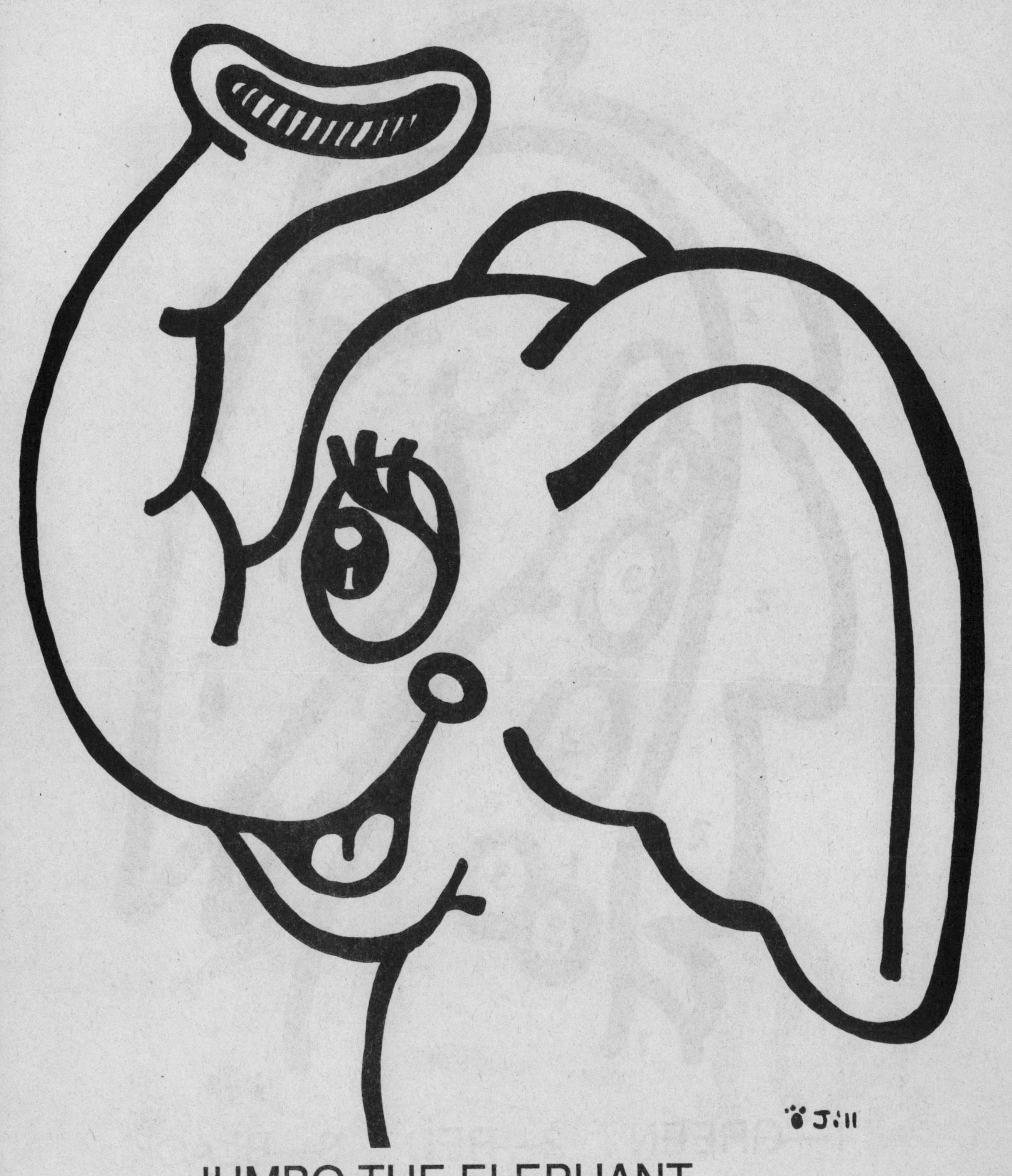

JUMBO THE ELEPHANT

2
1
2
3
3
3
2
1
1
1
3
2
1
3
3
1
1
Jill
1—GREEN 2—RED 3—BLACK

SLEEPY BABY

1—RED 2—GREEN 3—YELLOW 4—BLUE

UPSIDE DOWN BAT

HIPPITY HOP

COMETS HAVE A LONG TAIL

A DOLLAR TO SPEND

I'VE GOT CLAWS!

LITTLE JACK HORNER

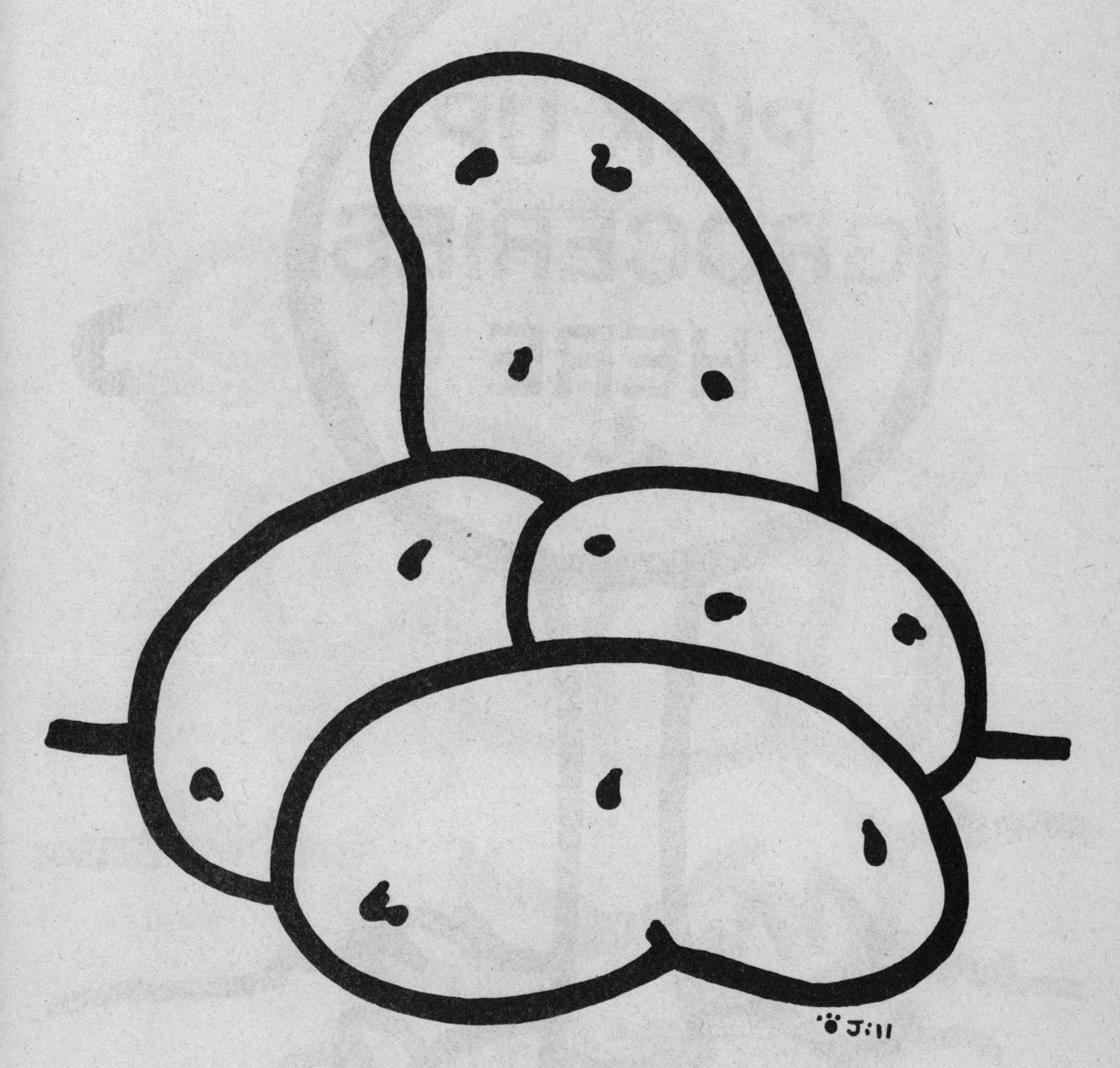

FOUR POTATOES

PICK-UP HERE!

THE GINGERBREAD MAN

POPCORN!

PAPA BEAR

ON A STRANGE PLANET

MALLARD DUCK

I'M LOST. HELP ME FIND
A WAY HOME.

THE UGLY DUCKLING...

HEN HOUSE

MARY HAD A LITTLE LAMB

BAKERY BREAD

ONLY 1 FOOT!

DELIVERY TRUCK

SOUR LEMONS

LEAP FROG

SCARY COBRA

MY HOUSE IS MADE OF STICKS.

THE SUN

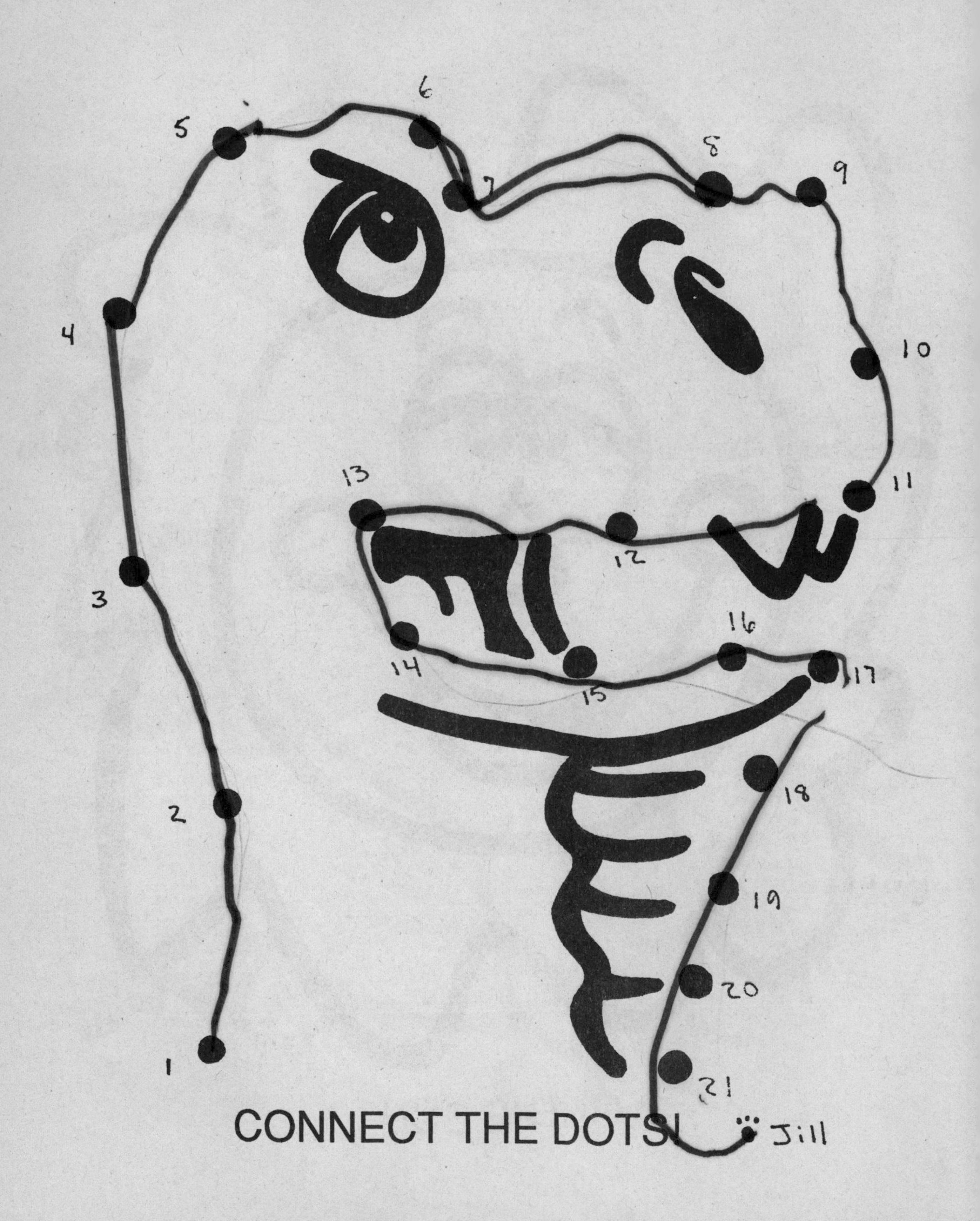

CONNECT THE DOTS! Jill

LONG DOG

BALLET SLIPPERS

JACK FELL DOWN!

SILLY RIDE!

ON THE MOON!

CIRCUS PIG

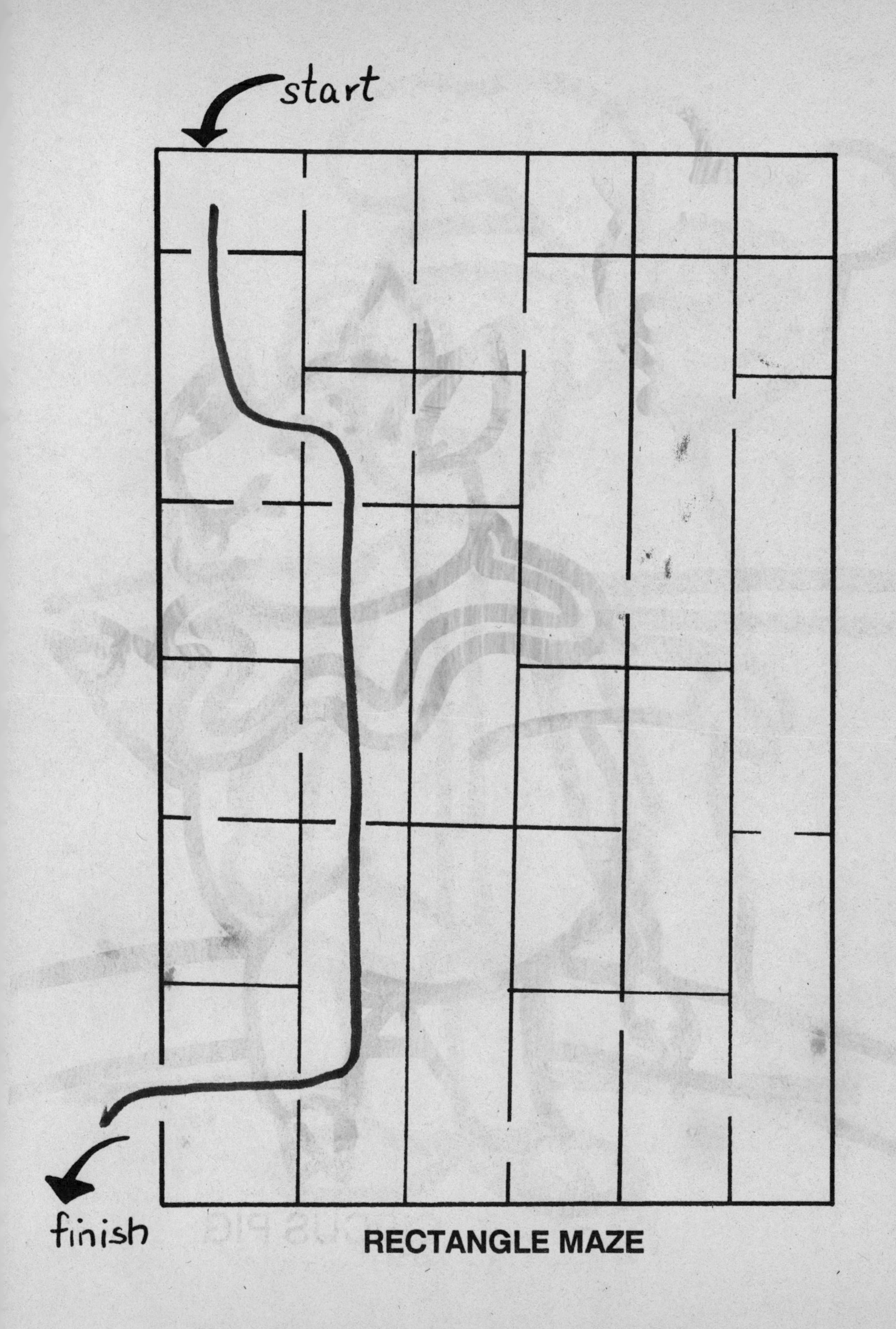

RECTANGLE MAZE

BILL THE BAKER

BABY FOOD

CHOCOLATE CHIP COOKIES

SNEAKY SNAKE

CUPCAKES
Jill

LEO LION

BOTTLE OF BLEACH

NUTTY FELLOW

MY BABY BUGGY

TAKING A WALK

LOTS OF TEETH!

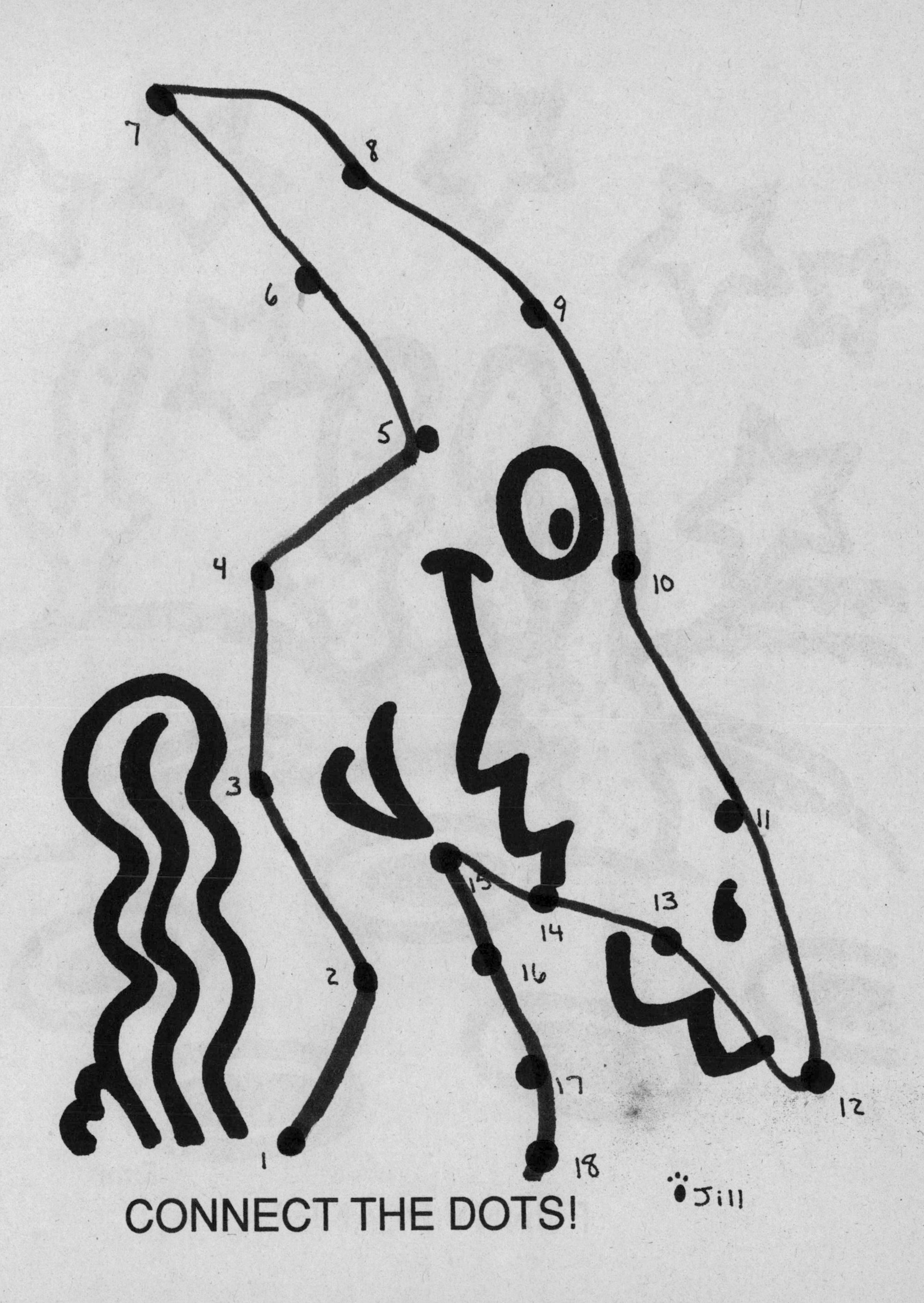

CONNECT THE DOTS!

FUNNY PLANET

COLOR THE CIRCUS HATS

I CAN FLY!

SPACE DOG

FEELING HIS OATS!

CIRCUS PONY

PERCY THE PIG

TRICK BEAR

TALL MAN

THE BRICK HOUSE!

TRAPEZE TRACY

GOLDILOCKS

SCARY TIGER

TEDDY RIDES IN THE CART WITH ME!

THREE KITTENS LOST THEIR MITTENS.

HAPPY SPRING!

PHIL THE FOX

CIRCUS WAGON

BIRTHDAY CAKE

PETEY PUP

SHY DEER

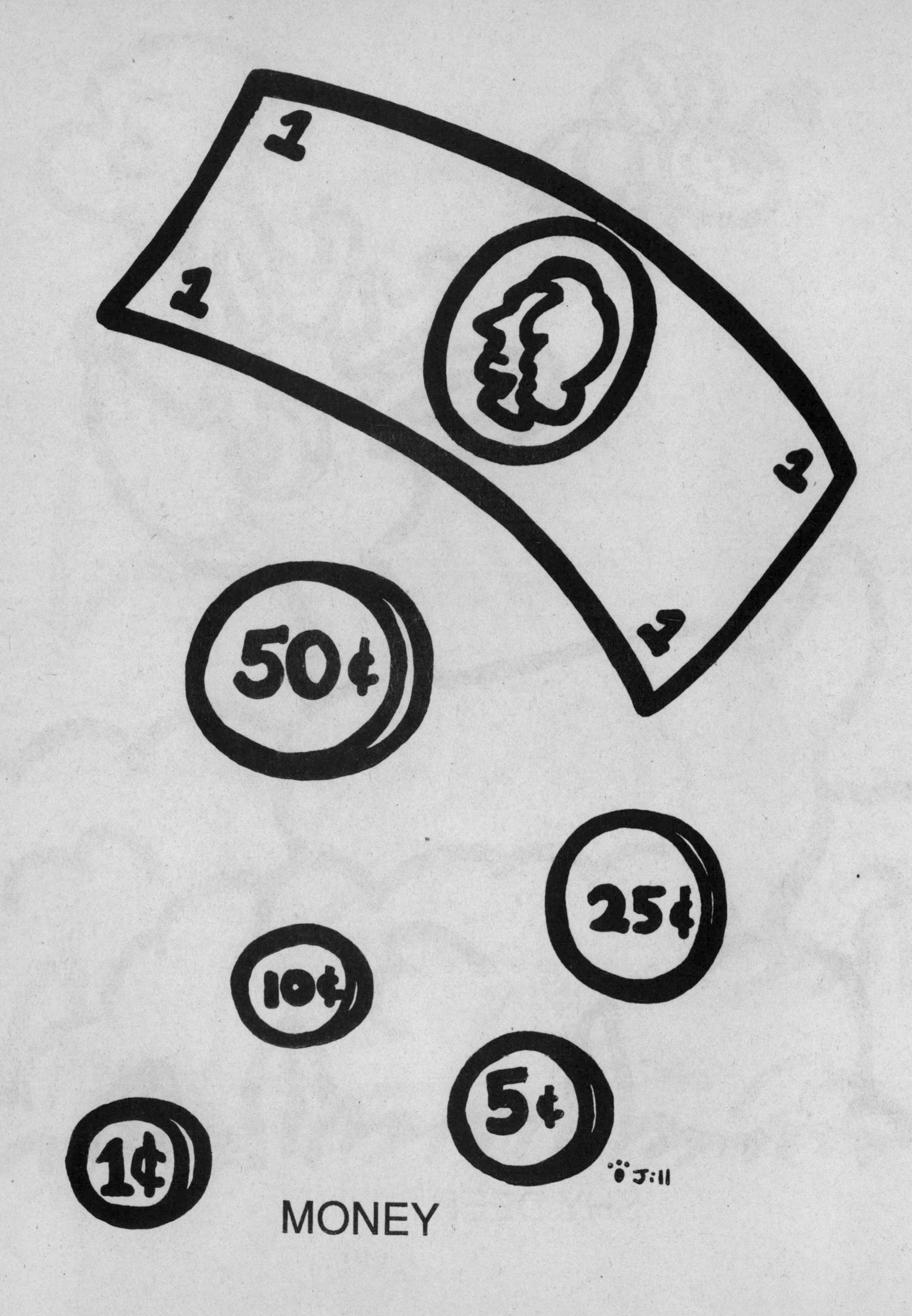

MONEY

MY NEW UMBRELLA

HIPPITY HOP

BABY PACIFIER

MOON AND STARS

FARMER BROWN

SHEP THE FARM DOG

SPACE ROCKET

SNEAKY RAT

CHUBBY ROOSTER

...TURNED INTO A SWAN!

ELEPHANT GIRL

IN SPACE

COTTON CANDY

MAGIC WAND

POTATO CHIPS

LITTLE BO PEEP

I'VE BEEN SHOPPING!

FIND THE FOSSIL

Jill

COUNT AND COLOR THE DOUGHNUTS

APPLE PIE!

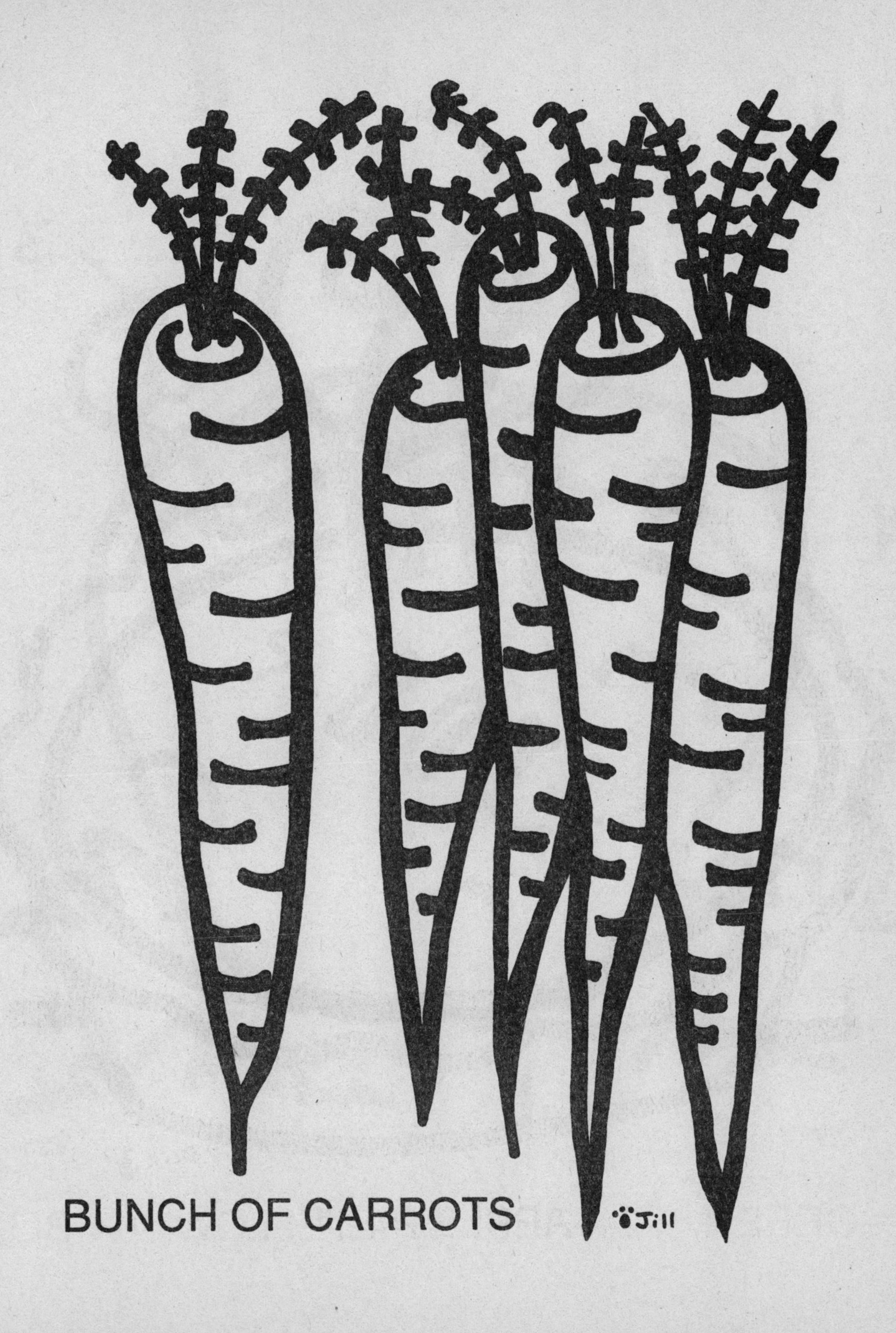

BUNCH OF CARROTS

1—GREEN 2—RED 3—YELLOW 4-BLUE

MY GRAMMY

SLEEPY BUNNY

LOUIE THE LOBSTER

LITTLE LAMB

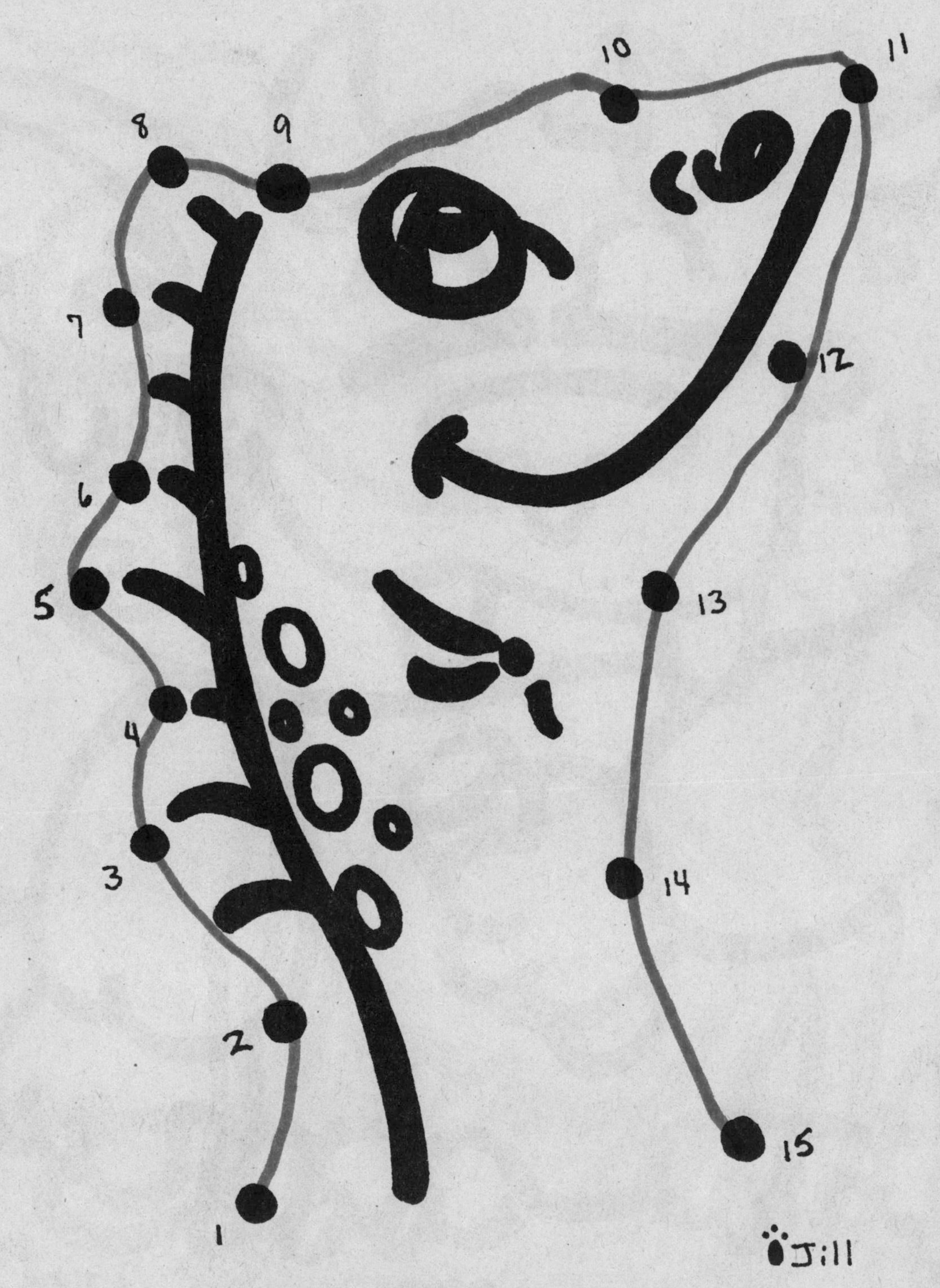

CONNECT THE DOTS!

I LIKE CANDY!!

THE DISH RAN AWAY WITH THE SPOON.

A PUMPKIN

DODO BIRD
Jill

LITTLE MISS MUFFET

MY HOUSE IS MADE OF BRICK!

DRAW LISA LION'S EYES

HOUSE MADE OF STRAW

HUMPTY DUMPTY

LITTLE BOY BLUE

UNCLE FRED'S TRACTOR

THE RINGMASTER

SHOPPING CART

BABY BEAR

TWINKLE, TWINKLE LITTLE STAR

CELERY

ICE CREAM CONE

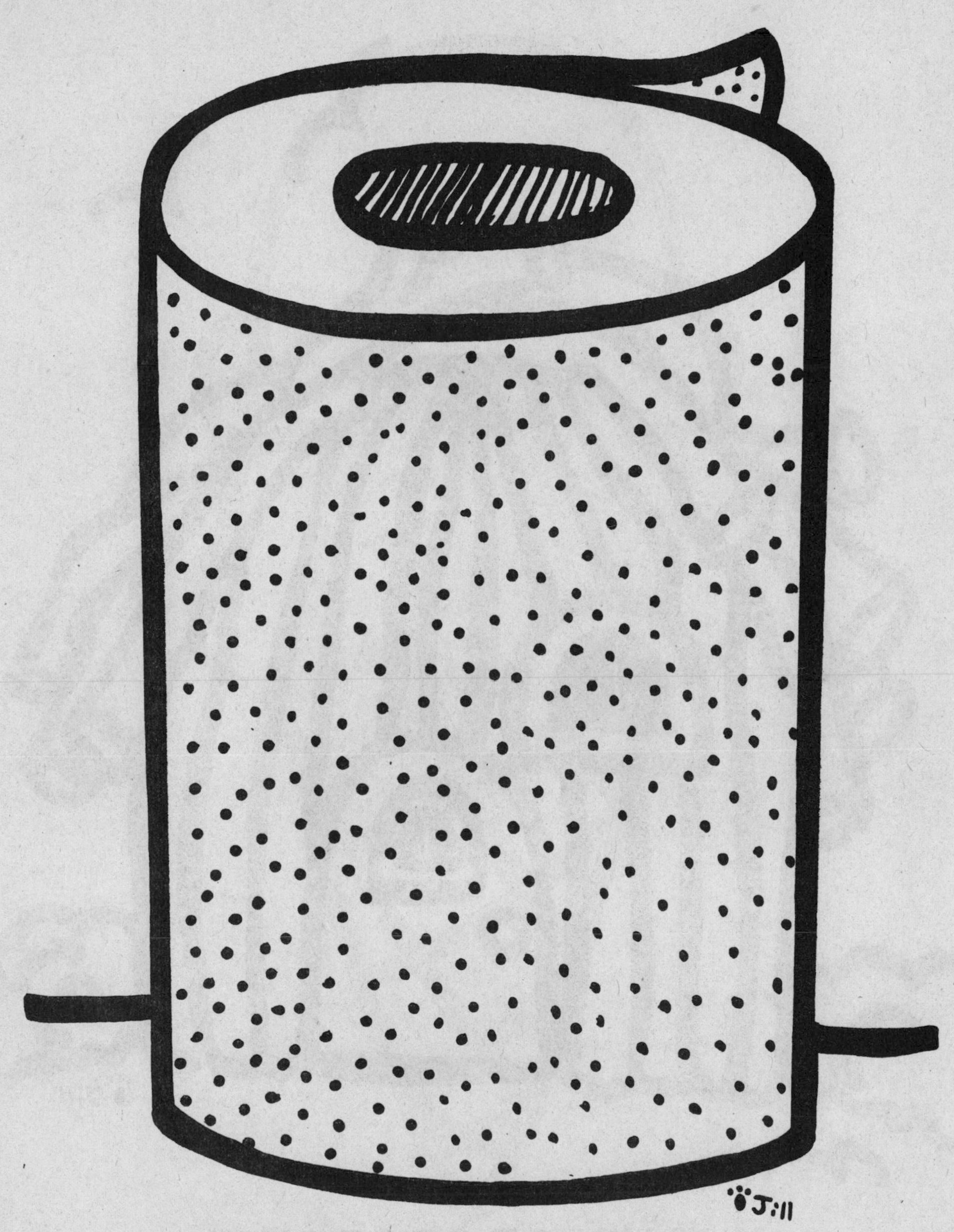

PAPER TOWEL ROLL

THE HOUSE OF STICKS

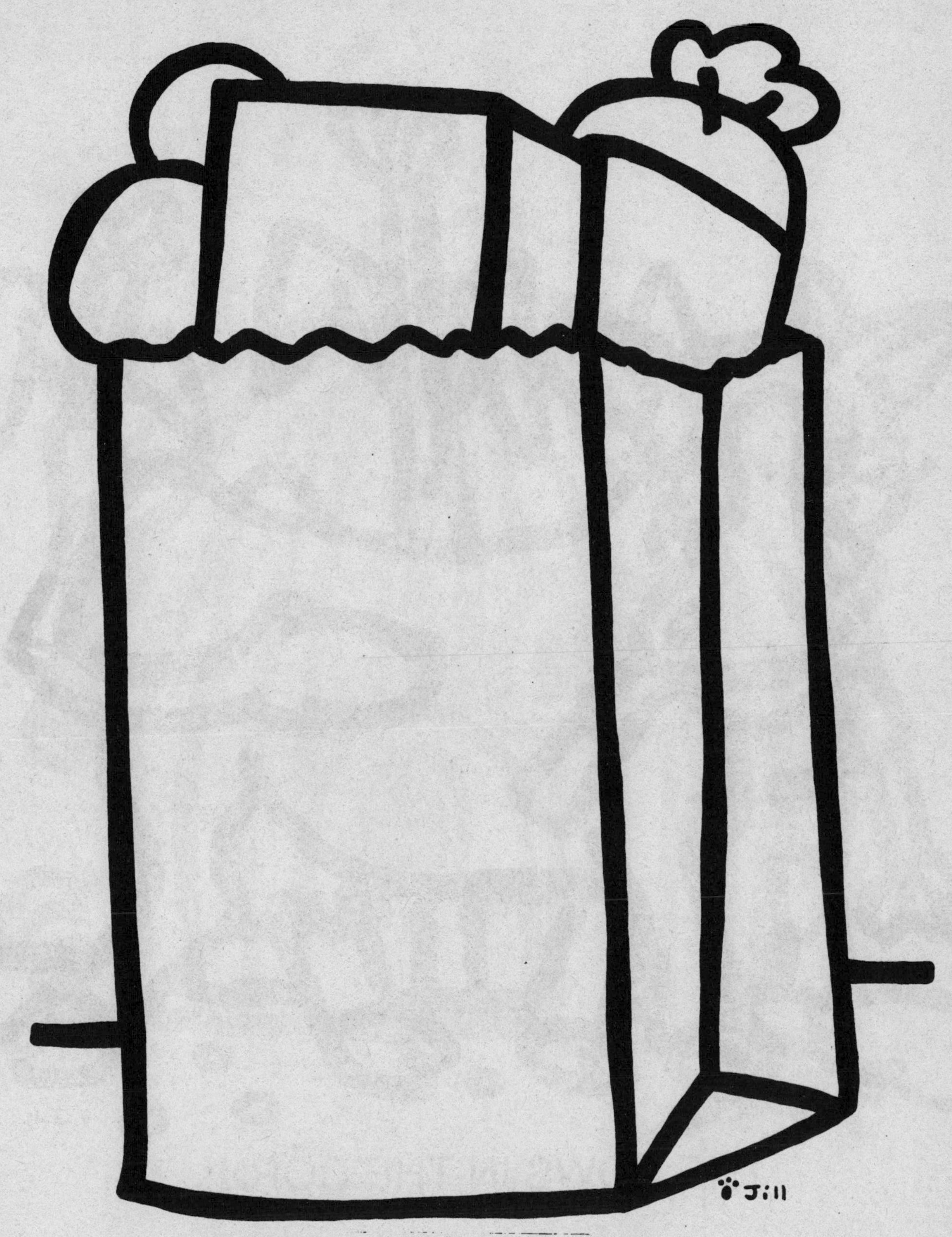

BAG OF GROCERIES

THE COWS IN THE CORN!

PLEASE DRAW MY LEGS.

MILK COMES FROM COWS

AL THE ALLIGATOR

WOODS DWELLER

DRAW BLINKY'S FACE

JUNGLE WALK

UP IN THE AIR

DRAW MY STRIPES

COUNT THE RAINDROPS ________

PLEASE ADDRESS MY LETTER

123456

MONKEY
AND
BANANA

12
1
2
3
4
5
6
7
8
9
10
11

SPACE DOG

THE CAT AND THE FIDDLE!

DAPPLE THE PONY

LOOK AT ME!

CIRCUS PONY

RED BARNS

JACKPOT
BAR
BAR
BAR

BOOM
BOOM
BOOM

CONNECT THE LINES AND DRAW THE PIG

CONNECT THE LINES TO DRAW TONY PONY

1 – BLUE 2 – BROWN 3 – RED
4 – YELLOW 5 – GREEN

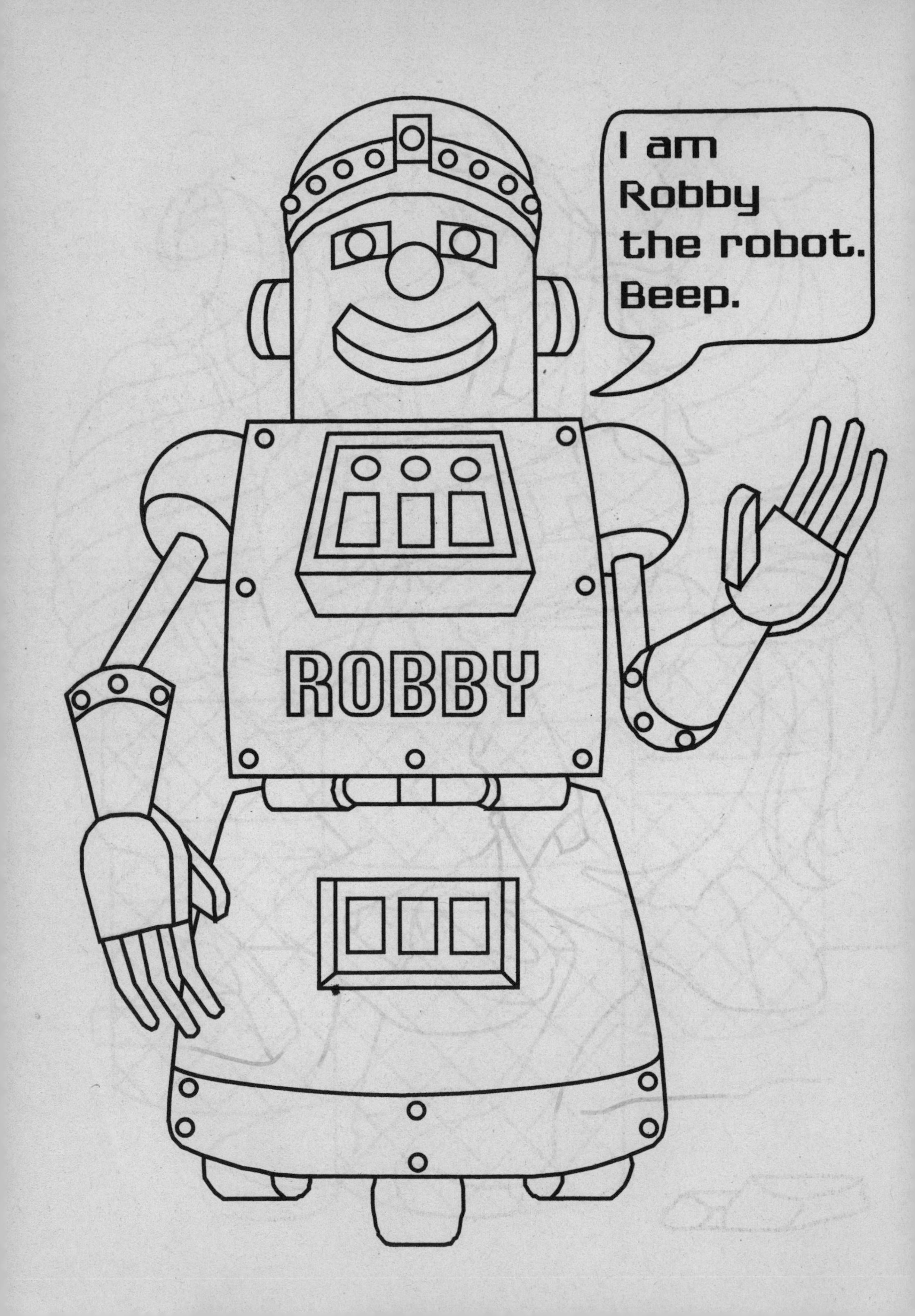
I am Robby the robot. Beep.
ROBBY

FIDO

1 — BLUE
2 — BLACK
3 — RED
4 — GREEN
5 — YELLOW
6 — BROWN
COLOR RANDY RACCOON BY NUMBER

COLOR ME BLACK

BILLY GOAT

BONNIE THE BEAR CUB

RAPUNZEL WAS LOCKED IN THE TOWER.